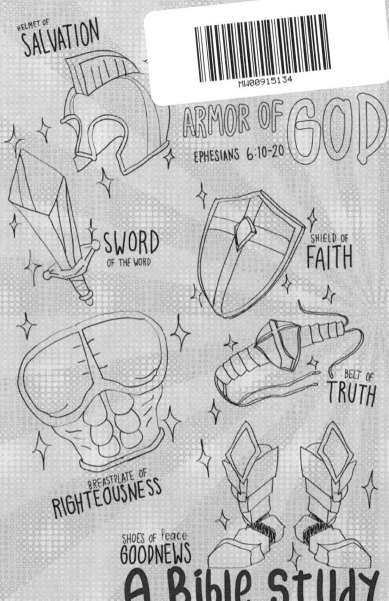

HELMET OF
SALVATION

ARMOR OF GOD
EPHESIANS 6:10-20

SWORD
OF THE WORD

SHIELD OF
FAITH

BELT OF
TRUTH

BREASTPLATE OF
RIGHTEOUSNESS

SHOES OF Peace
GOODNEWS

A Bible Study FOR Kids

BY: Mandy Fender

THIS BOOK BELONGS TO:

CONTENTS:

Put on the full armor of God, so that you can take your stand against the devil's schemes. For our struggle is not against flesh and blood, but against the rulers, against the authorities, against the powers of this dark world and against the spiritual forces of evil in the heavenly realms. Therefore put on the full armor of God, so that when the day of evil comes, you may be able to stand your ground, and after you have done everything, to stand. Stand firm then, with the belt of truth buckled around your waist, with the breastplate of righteousness in place, and with your feet fitted with the readiness that comes from the gospel of peace. In addition to all this, take up the shield of faith, with which you can extinguish all the flaming arrows of the evil one. Take the helmet of salvation and the sword of the Spirit, which is the word of God.

Ephesians 6:11-17 (NIV)

THE ARMOR OF GOD

THE ARMOR OF GOD

Devotions & Prayers

For the weapons of our warfare are not carnal, but mighty through God to the pulling down of strongholds.

2 CORINTHIANS 10:4

The Belt Of Truth

Stand firm then, with the belt of truth buckled around your waist...(Ephesians 6:14)

Protects:

THOUGHTS — helps you think clearly
HEART — guards your heart against lies
LIFE — helps you navigate life

Stats:

2 Timothy 2:15, John 14:6, Psalm 25:5, John 16:13

John 8:31–32 (NIV)

Jesus said, "If you hold to my teaching, you are really my disciples. Then you will know the truth, and the truth will set you free."

Jesus wants us to hold on to what He says, because everything He says is true, for He is the way, the truth, and the life. In 2 Timothy 2:15, the Bible instructs us to study the Word of God and rightly divide the truth, meaning we should ask God's help to understand His Word.

Understanding the Bible can be hard sometimes, even for adults, but the Spirit of God will help us learn and understand the words we read as we read them. The most important truth we have is JESUS! The truth is: Jesus came to save that which was lost and all who call upon the name of the Lord will be saved. Believe in Him, trust Him, and follow Him.

PRAYER:

Lord, help me keep the Belt of Truth on and lead me as I live my life. May Your truth be found in my heart and mind. I pray for understanding as I read Your Word. In Jesus' name, amen!

QUESTIONS:

Where can we find the truth?
What can we do with the truth?
How does the truth of God's Word help you?

.:Notes:.

.:Notes:.

The Breastplate of Righteousness

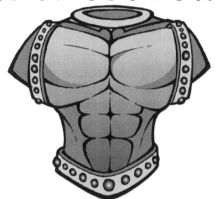

with the breastplate of righteousness in place...(Ephesians 6:14)

Protects:

HEART — helps keep your heart safe from evil
ACTIONS — helps you make the right choices
MOTIVES — helps you do right for the right reasons

Stats:

Proverbs 21:3, 2 Timothy 3:16, 1 John 2:29

PROVERbS 4:23 (NIV)

Above all else, guard your heart,
for everything you do flows from it.

What part of the body does a breastplate cover? The heart and major organs! Righteousness helps us guard our hearts, because when we do right, we do not have to lie or hide. The Bible says in Proverbs that the righteous are as bold as lions, but the wicked flee when no one is chasing. Why do you think the wicked flee even when no one is chasing? Because they know they are wrong. But, a person who does right before the Lord can have a clear heart and mind.

God has given us everything we need to live a life that is righteous through Jesus Christ. We can now be forgiven, set free, and made whole through Him!

PRAYER:

Lord, thank You for the Breastplate of Righteousness. Guard my heart and help me to do right and make the right choices, even if they're hard. In Jesus' name, amen!

QUESTIONS:

What do you think it means to be righteous?
What are some things you can do that you know are right?
Who does our righteousness come from?

.:Notes:.

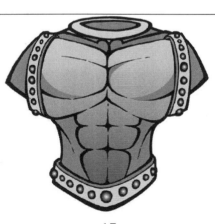

.:Notes:.

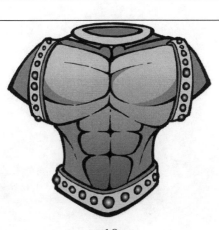

Shoes of Peace

...and with your feet fitted with the readiness that comes from the gospel of peace.
(Ephesians 6:15)

Protects:

DIRECTION – helps us not be moved
HEART – helps our hearts be strong
MIND – gives us a sound mind

Stats:
Job 22: 21-22, Psalm 4:8, Luke 1: 78-79

ISAIAH 52:7 (NIV)

How beautiful on the mountains
are the feet of those who bring good news,
who proclaim peace,
who bring good tidings,
who proclaim salvation,
who say to Zion,
"Your God reigns!"

Jesus said He gives us peace and, not just any peace, but His peace. His peace is secure and is not moved by what happens in this world. In this world, trouble happens, but Jesus has given us His Word so that we might find peace through it all. Remember, God wants you to have peace at all times and in every way. Give Jesus your worries and fears and let Him be the peace you need.

The peace and good news we have should be shared with others! We can share peace by being peaceful with others, by speaking words of peace, and by acting in peace. Do your best to be peaceful at home, at church, and at school!

PRAYER:
Lord, I pray for Shoes of Peace. Let me have the courage to share the good news of Your peace with others, too. In Jesus' name, amen!

QUESTIONS:
What do you think peace is?
How can you share the good news of God's peace?
Where does our peace come from?

.:Notes:.

_____

_____

_____

_____

_____

_____

_____

_____

_____

_____

_____

_____

_____

_____

_____

_____

_____

_____

_____

.:Notes:.

Shield of faith

In addition to all this, take up the shield of faith, with which you can extinguish all the flaming arrows of the evil one. (Ephesians 6:16)

Protects:

WHOLE
BODY – helps our mind, body, and soul
LIFE – guides and protects our entire life

Stats:

2 Corinthians 5:7, James 1:6, Hebrews 11:6

HEBREWS 11:1 (NKJV)

Now faith is the substance of things hoped for, the evidence of things not seen.

Faith is all about what we believe and who we believe in. What we believe will guide our lives, choices, and words we speak. The Bible says faith is what we hope for, but cannot see. What is our hope? Our hope is in Jesus Christ, who He is, and what He has done.

The Bible even says faith can move mountains! Having faith means trusting Jesus and relying on Him. At times, you will have to fight for your faith, because what you believe is always being tested. But, if you keep your eyes and focus on Jesus, He will help you grow your faith. The more time we spend doing the things of God, the more our faith increases, and it is faith in Jesus Christ that helps us overcome! Start using your Shield of Faith in everything you do! In the Bible, people used their faith in extraordinary ways, be brave and use your faith, too!

PRAYER:
Lord, I pray that I keep my faith in You. Help me to use my Shield of Faith in great ways! In Jesus' name, amen!

QUESTIONS:
What can you do to build your faith?
How can you use your faith?
Where can you use your faith?

.:Notes:.

.:Notes:.

Helmet of Salvation

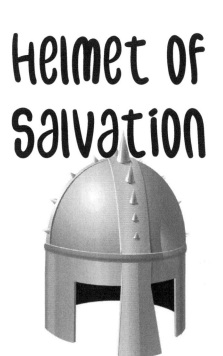

Take the helmet of salvation... (Ephesians 6:17)

Protects:

MIND — gives us a new way of thinking
THOUGHTS — transforms our thoughts
WORDS — helps us guard what we say

Stats:

John 3:16, Romans 1:16, Titus 2: 11-14

Isaiah 12:2 (NIV)

Surely God is my salvation; I will trust and not be afraid. The LORD, the LORD himself, is my strength and my defense; he has become my salvation.

What part of the body does a helmet protect? The head, that's right! God has given us the HELMET OF SALVATION to help protect our minds, thoughts, and words. Salvation comes through Jesus Christ. The Bible says we are saved by grace through faith in Jesus (Ephesians 2:8-9).

Salvation makes us new and gives us a new way of thinking. We can pray for wisdom and renew our minds through God's Word. We can now have the mind of Christ and that will help our thoughts and our words. Every word, before it is spoken, is first a thought; use the helmet before you speak. This helmet will help you filter thoughts and words!

PRAYER:
Lord, I pray for the mind of Christ and that the Helmet of Salvation helps me with my thoughts and words. In Jesus' name, amen!

QUESTIONS:
Who is your salvation?
Can you find and read John 3:16?
What does the Helmet of Salvation protect?

.:Notes:.

.:Notes:.

SWORD OF the SPIRIT, THE WORD OF GOD

...and the sword of the Spirit, which is the word of God. (Ephesians 6:17)

PROTECTS:

WHOLE
BODY – can be offensive and defensive
LIFE — helps us in every way

Stats:

Psalm 119:105, Hebrews 4:12, John 1:1

2 Timothy 3:16-17 (NIV)

All Scripture is God-breathed and is useful for teaching, rebuking, correcting and training in righteousness, so that the servant of God may be thoroughly equipped for every good work.

The Word is powerful and comes straight from God. We have the Word to help us with every part of our lives. The Word gives us instructions and teaches us right from wrong, and good from bad. The Word is like a map we can use to help us find our way.

In good times, the Bible tells us to praise God. In bad times, the Bible tells us to trust God. For every season we go through, the Word is there to help us, inspire us, and encourage us. God's Word stands the test of time and will always be the truth we need. The Word of the Lord remains forever!

Prayer:

Lord, thank You for the Sword of the Spirit. I pray I hide the Word in my heart so that I always remember it and live by it. In Jesus' name, amen!

Questions:

What is your favorite Bible Verse?
What is your favorite Bible story?
How can you use the Word of God in your life?

.:Notes:.

_____
_____
_____
_____
_____
_____
_____
_____
_____
_____
_____
_____
_____
_____
_____
_____
_____
_____
_____
_____

.:Notes:.

THE ARMOR OF GOD

Bible Research

Finally, be strong in the Lord and in his mighty power.

ePHeSIaNS 6:10

BIBLE VERSES:

*Write Down One
Verse in Each Box*

BIBLE VERSES:

*Write Down One
Verse in Each Box*

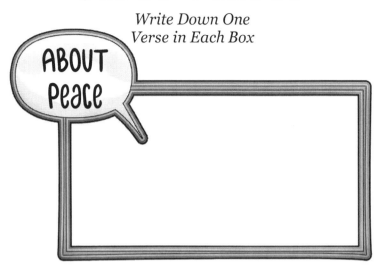

BiBLe VeRSeS:

*Write Down One
Verse in Each Box*

STRENGTHEN YOUR ARMOR

*For the **Word of God** is quick, and powerful, and sharper than any two-edged sword, piercing even to the dividing asunder of soul and spirit, and of the joints and marrow, and is a discerner of the thoughts and intents of the heart.*

Hebrews 4:12

All scripture is given by inspiration of God, and is profitable for doctrine, for reproof, for correction, for instruction in righteousness...

2 Timothy 3:16

Reading the Bible, memorizing Bible verses, and putting that knowledge into action helps you follow Jesus and live life like He wants you to. On the next few pages, write down Bible verses that you would like to memorize to strengthen your armor.

BIBLE VERSES I WANT TO MEMORIZE:

BIBLE VERSES I WANT TO MEMORIZE:

BIBLE VERSES I WANT TO MEMORIZE:

BIBLE VERSES I WANT TO MEMORIZE:

THE ARMOR OF GOD

FUN ACTIVITIES

I the Lord search the heart...

JEREMIAH 17:10

DRAW

YOUR

ARMOR

On the next six pages, draw each piece of the
Armor of God.

Be creative!

This is MY Belt Of TRuth

This is my Breastplate of Righteousness

These are My Shoes of Peace

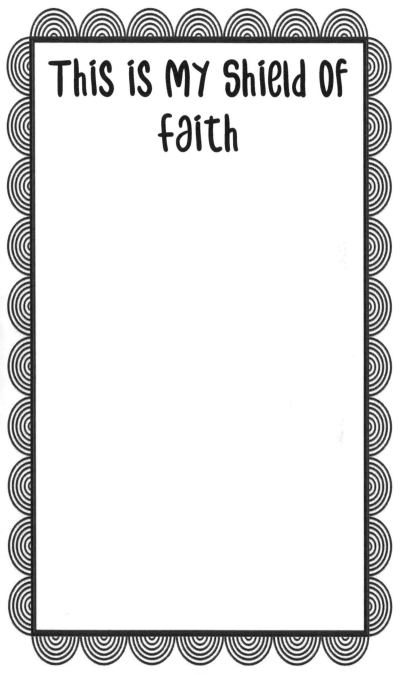

This is My Shield Of Faith

This is My Helmet of Salvation

THiS iS MY SWORD OF the SPiRit

This is My Full Armor of God

Draw yourself wearing the Full Armor of God.

Blessed is the one who perseveres under trial because, having stood the test, that person will receive the crown of life that the Lord has promised to those who love him.

JAMES 1:12

THE ARMOR OF GOD

Challenge Time

Challenge

Your

Memory

Can you remember each piece of armor?

Can you identify and name each piece of the Armor of God?

DO YOU accept the Challenge?

Challenge Accepted

WE WILL START OFF EASY...

HOW MANY PIECES
OF ARMOR ARE
THERE?

_ _ _ _ _

6

CORRECT!

Without looking back, list the

ARMOR OF GOD:

1_____

2_____

3_____

4_____

5_____

6_____

THE WHOLE ARMOR OF GOD

EPHESIANS 6:10-20

HELMET OF SALVATION

SWORD OF THE WORD

SHIELD OF FAITH

BELT OF TRUTH

BREASTPLATE OF RIGHTEOUSNESS

SHOES of PEACE GOODNEWS

Did YOU get them Right?

IDENTIFY BY Sight

Without looking, identify and name each piece of the Armor of God.

THE ARMOR OF GOD

FINAL THOUGHTS

Good and upright is
the Lord...
PSALM 25:8

What I Learned

Write at least 1 thing you learned in each bubble.

MY ThOUghts

What I Learned

Write at least 1 thing you learned in each bubble.

MY THOUGHTS

HOW I WILL USE the ARMOR OF GOD IN MY LIFE

On the next few pages, write down how you will use each piece of the Armor of God in your daily life.

MY ThOUGhts

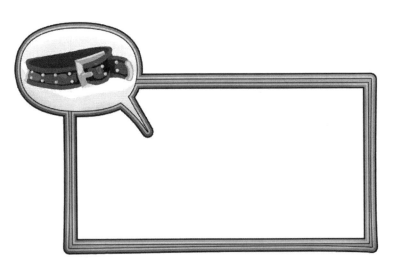

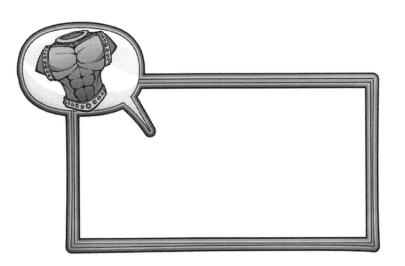

MY ThOUghts

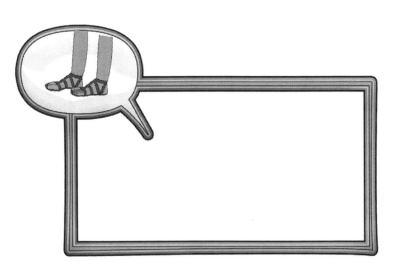

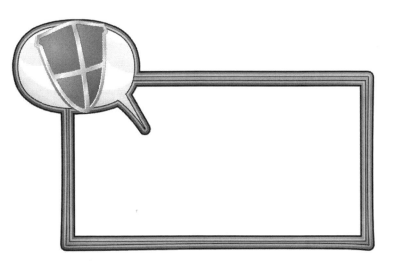

MY ThOUghts

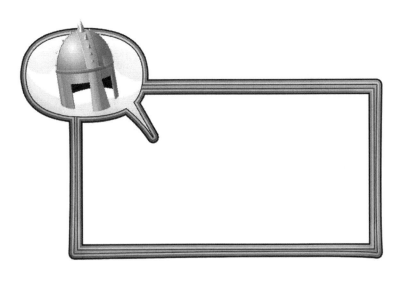

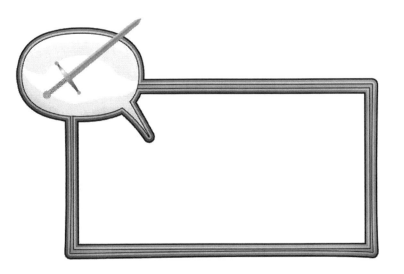

MY THOUGHTS

MY Favorite Piece Of Armor to Learn About Was:

Because:

MY ThOUGhTS

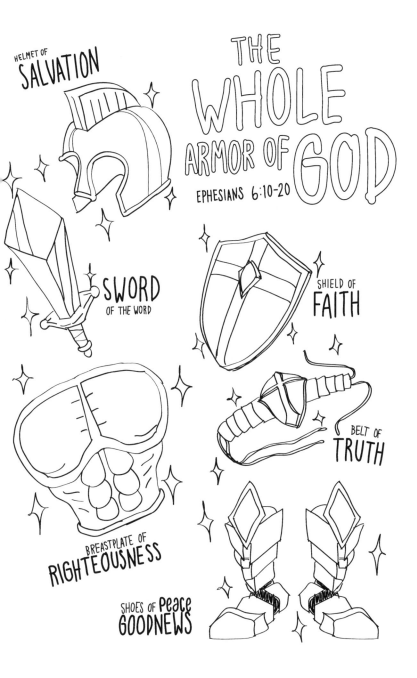

HELMET OF
SALVATION

THE
WHOLE
ARMOR OF GOD
EPHESIANS 6:10-20

SWORD
OF THE WORD

SHIELD OF
FAITH

BELT OF
TRUTH

BREASTPLATE OF
RIGHTEOUSNESS

SHOES OF Peace
GOODNEWS

Peace to the brothers and sisters, and love with faith from God the Father and the Lord Jesus Christ. Grace to all who love our Lord Jesus Christ with an undying love.

Ephesians 6:23–24

Thank you so much for reading!
May you be greatly blessed and
always remember to wear the
FULL ARMOR OF GOD!

Blessings,

Mandy Fender

Made in the USA
Middletown, DE
26 November 2024

65478092R00057